Leader's Guide ❧ ❧ ❧ ❧ ❧ ❧ ❧ ❧ ❧ ❧ ❧ ❧

Guided Meditations for Junior High

A QUIET PLACE APART

Leader's Guide 🙰🙰🙰🙰🙰🙰🙰🙰🙰🙰🙰

Guided Meditations for Junior High: Good Judgment, Gifts, Obedience, Inner Blindness

Jane E. Ayer

Saint Mary's Press
Christian Brothers Publications
Winona, Minnesota

Genuine recycled paper with 10% post-consumer waste.
Printed with soy-based ink.

The publishing team included Robert P. Stamschror, development editor;
Jacqueline M. Captain, manuscript editor; Alan S. Hanson, typesetter;
Maurine R. Twait, art director; Karen J. Doyle, illustrator; cover photo
copyright © 1996 PhotoDisc, Inc.; pre-press, printing, and binding by the
graphics division of Saint Mary's Press.

The acknowledgments continue on page 45.

Printed in the United States of America

Printing: 9 8 7 6 5 4 3 2

Year: 2005 04 03 02

ISBN 0-88489-500-9

Contents

To my parents
whose leap into Catholic conversion
rooted me in my faith . . .
thank you!

Directions for Leading the Meditations

LEADER PREPARATION

As the meditation leader, your preparation is especially important to the success of a guided meditation. Pray the meditation before leading a group in it. This will help you to become comfortable with its style and content. Some materials may require a brief doctrinal review with the group. By praying the meditation first, you will become aware if there is a need to do this.

If you choose to have your group do the optional art expression as follow-up to the meditations, it is best if you try it out before the group gathers to make sure it works well for you and to know better what directions to give.

If you intend to guide the meditations yourself rather than use the accompanying cassette or compact disc, rehearse the guided prayer, including the introductory comments, the scriptural reading, and the opening and closing prayers, so that appropriate and sufficient time is allowed for the imagery to take place and for prayerful reflection to occur. The meditations should be read slowly and prayerfully, using soft instrumental music as a background.

Only a good reader who has prepared should read aloud the scriptural passage that precedes each guided meditation. The scriptural passage is important to establishing the theme and the tone of the meditation. Read it with reverence and expression, using a Bible.

PARTICIPANT PREPARATION

To introduce praying a guided meditation, it might be helpful to explain that the participants will be using a prayer form that will call upon their imagination, and that the

Holy Spirit graces our imagination during prayer to help us to communicate with God. Remember that this type of prayer may not be easy for everyone in the group. Some may be self-conscious about closing their eyes; some may have difficulty getting in touch with their feelings; some might have personal obstacles in their relationship with the Lord. Be gentle, let go, and let the Spirit work. In fact, participants can be told that although the meditation is guided, if the Spirit leads them in another direction, it is okay for them to go with their own reflection and not worry about the words being spoken.

A possible difficulty, one that may not be apparent at first, may be encountered by those who wear the type of contact lenses that prevent them from closing their eyes for an extended period of time. Invite these participants to put their head down, hiding their eyes in the dark crook of their arm, if they are unable to remove the lenses. Another possible difficulty may be experienced by those who have a sinus problem or asthma. Instead of breathing through their nose during the deep-breathing exercises, they can breathe quietly through their mouth.

MUSIC Quiet instrumental music is important for setting and keeping the mood of the meditation. Music can be playing even as the group gathers. It is a nice background for giving instructions. Have additional tapes or compact discs ready to play during the activities after the guided meditation. Ideally, the follow-up activities will take place in a separate space; therefore, it is less disruptive if cassette or CD players are already set up in the different areas.

REFLECTION Allowing time for the participants to reflect and name the
QUESTIONS experience they have just gone through is a necessary part of these prayer experiences. The reflection questions will help the participants do this successfully. Choose several reflection questions (or use questions similar to them) and type them up, leaving room after each for a response. Make a copy for each participant. Allot enough time for each person

to respond to the questions and to share his or her responses with the group. These prayer experiences are not meant to be rushed.

To avoid disrupting the quiet mood of the meditation time, pass out the reflection questions (placed facedown) as the participants take their places. Also give a pen or pencil to each person. If people are sitting on the floor, you could give out hardcover books or clipboards to facilitate writing. Explain that you are distributing reflection questions for use after the meditation.

Assure the participants that their responses are private and that their papers are not going to be collected. When it is time for sharing, honor and affirm all responses, and respect those persons who do not wish to answer aloud.

ART EXPRESSION (OPTIONAL)

Each prayer experience comes with an optional art expression. You might choose to use this rather than the reflection questions.

If you choose to do an optional art expression, prepare the art materials ahead of time and lay them out in the area where the participants will work. Familiarize the group with the art activity before the prayer time, if possible, so as not to disrupt the meditation mood. This should allow you to give particular directions for the art activity without having to answer a lot of questions. If you have previously completed the art expression, it might be helpful to show your sample artwork at this time.

SETTING

It is imperative that the area for the prayer experience is quiet—no ringing of telephones, bells, and the like. If necessary, put a sign on the outside of your door: Praying! Please do not disturb!

Participants may sit in chairs or find a comfortable position on the floor, but they must be a few feet from one another so that they each have their own space and do not distract one another. Therefore, the area must be large enough so the participants are not cramped. Lying down on the floor should be discouraged, as some participants are likely to fall asleep.

CENTERPIECE
(OPTIONAL)

Each theme of the prayer experiences can be enhanced by creating a centerpiece that can be placed on a small table, an altar, or the middle of the floor. The centerpiece should include objects that reflect the message of the prayer. For example, for the meditation on good judgment ("Choose Wisely"), you might display a sword and a baby doll laid on a purple cloth, the color of royalty. You could have a scale to imply justice, or a poster divided in half with the word "Yes" on one side and the word "No" written on the other. Include candles and a Bible opened to the scriptural passage.

To enhance the meditation on gifts ("Don't Bury Them"), the centerpiece might consist of a treasure chest effect with a decorated box, "gold coins" or loose change, and costume jewelry strewn over a draped cloth with candles and an open Bible. A mirror could also be used to depict the reflection of the gift of each individual.

A centerpiece for the meditation on obedience ("Do It Willingly") might include some wheat, hay, or grapes to depict the fields and a framed photo of someone's parents. (Or you could suggest ahead of time that everyone bring in a picture of their parents, guardians, or family.) Candles and an open Bible should be included.

To set the theme for the meditation on inner blindness ("I Want to See"), the centerpiece might display a tattered cloak or sweater, sunglasses, a blindfold or mask, a white cane or walking stick, candles, and an open Bible.

MATERIALS NEEDED
FOR EACH
MEDITATION

- a Bible
- an audiotape or CD player
- the meditation recording or script
- tapes or CDs of instrumental music
- reflection questions (a copy for each participant)
- pens or pencils
- clipboards or hardcover books to facilitate writing, if needed
- materials for the art expression (optional; see individual project's needs)
- a centerpiece to reflect the theme (optional)
- a sign that reads Praying! Please do not disturb!

Good Judgment ∽∽∽∽∽∽∽∽∽∽
Choose Wisely

This enlightening prayer experience, "Choose Wisely," is based on Solomon's good judgment. It calls us to be like Solomon in our personal decision making and in our dealings with others.

THEME After you have given directions to the participants and set the tone for meditation, introduce the theme by saying something like the following:

> It is important for us to spend time in a quiet place apart so that we can think about the judgments we have made and the judgments we need to make. We need to take time out so that we can be wise like Solomon and make choices that are good for ourselves and others. We can help this to happen in the hush of our quiet place.

OPENING   Read aloud this opening prayer:

> Dear Lord, help us to become comfortable with this quiet time so that we can visit with you and talk about some of the decisions we have made or need to make. Give us the grace to openly face the choices that confront our lives so that we can make good judgments by choosing wisely. Amen.

SCRIPTURE   Read aloud 1 Kings 3:16–28, using a Bible.

SCRIPT   Play the "Choose Wisely" meditation on the accompanying recording or slowly and reverently read aloud the following script for the guided meditation. Play soft, instrumental background music.

> Today you will enter the hush of your quiet place and meet Jesus in your imagination. First, you will begin by doing some deep-breathing exercises. When I say to, if you can, breathe in and out through your nose quietly during these exercises. Close your eyes and get comfortable. You will be relaxing your entire body.
>
> Breathe in deeply . . . hold it . . . breathe out slowly and completely. Breathe in deeply . . . hold it . . . breathe out slowly and completely. Again, breathe in deeply . . . hold it . . . breathe out slowly and completely.
>
> Allow your feet and ankles to relax. . . . Relax your legs . . . and your hips. . . . Remember to keep breathing in deeply and out slowly. Relax your stomach muscles . . . and now your chest. . . . Just relax. . . . Let your arms grow limp. . . . Relax your wrists, . . . your hands, . . . and your fingers. . . . Stay mindful of your breathing.

Allow your shoulders to become heavy. . . .
Let all the tension drain from your shoulders. . . .
Relax your neck, . . . your facial muscles, . . .
and even your eyelids. . . . Just relax. . . .
Breathe in deeply . . . hold it . . . breathe out
slowly and completely. [Pause.]

You are safely sitting in an empty movie
theater, wondering what you are doing there, when
you hear someone calling out your name. . . .
You turn and look. . . . It is someone you recog-
nize. . . . It is Jesus. Again, he calls out your name
in greeting as he comes down the aisle toward you.
. . . He is smiling and looks very happy to see you.
. . . Jesus sits down next to you and seems very
relaxed to be there in the cinema with you. . . .
Hear Jesus tell you that he is glad that you are here
and that he wants you to watch something with
him. . . . He tells you that it is something that
happened a long time ago. . . . You settle back in
your chair like you usually do in the movies. . . .

You watch the big screen. You see a king with
two very agitated women. . . . Jesus whispers to
you that the king is Solomon and that he has a very
difficult decision to make. . . . One of the women
is holding a baby who is crying. . . . She is doing
nothing to comfort the child, but she is holding
very tightly to this bundle in her arms. . . . The
other woman's face is wet with tears and her hands
are clenched together in front of her chest. . . .
You can hear that the music playing in the background is hauntingly sad but then it picks up tem-
po as the two women argue. . . .

The woman with the baby is angry and shouting at the king. Hear her say: "The baby is mine! . . .

She can't have him! Tell her so! . . . I'll pay you whatever you want. . . ." The tear-stained face of the other woman looks at the king and says quietly but insistently: "He is my son. . . . Do not take him from me. . . ." Except for the cries of the baby, silence fills the room. Both women now seem to be waiting for the king to speak.

Watch as King Solomon looks at both women. . . . In a powerful voice, hear him call, "Guards!" Two men come quickly to his side. King Solomon continues in a very authoritative voice: "Cut the baby in half and give half to each of these women here. Do it at once. . . ."

The music from the movie is becoming loud and scary. . . . You watch as the guards grab hold of the baby boy. . . . One guard raises a very nasty-looking sword. . . . The woman who has been crying all along now falls to her knees and cries out to the king: "Your majesty, please do not harm one hair on the head of my son. . . . You may give him to this woman rather than have him killed. . . ." The woman's voice is very brave, but it does not stop the tears from flowing down her cheeks. . . . The other woman's face is gloating. . . . She thinks that she has won. She puts her arms out to take the infant. . . . The guards ignore her. . . .

But now when King Solomon reaches for the baby, the guards immediately hand him over. . . . You wonder what this great king's decision will be. You can almost feel the tension from that room. . . . Notice what you are feeling when he gently passes the baby boy to the kneeling woman. . . . Her head is still bowed so low that she doesn't even know he is doing this until the baby reaches out and grabs playfully for her hair. . . . Startled, she looks up; overjoyed and grateful, she receives the child from the king. . . . Notice the music soften-ing in the background. . . . The king speaks: "You are the true and rightful mother. . . . No real mother would stand by and see her child split in two. . . . Go and raise him well. . . ." You look at the other woman's face. It is red and filled with anger. . . . You suspect that it is only from her losing to the other woman and not from any real caring about the infant. The king turns to her: "You are a wretched woman. Get out of my sight. . . ."

Now Jesus turns toward you. . . . He asks you what you have thought of Solomon's decision. . . . Take a moment and share with Jesus your feelings and thoughts about what just happened. . . . Jesus tells you he believes that Solomon was wise because he thought before he acted. . . . He asks you to share with him your wise decisions—decisions that you have made that you have been proud of. Think a moment and then tell Jesus what you have said or done at home or school, at church or anywhere, whether among friends, family, strang-ers, or alone that has made you feel good about yourself. [Pause.]

Hear Jesus tell you how much he appreciates the good decisions that you have made. [Pause.]

Jesus leans in toward you and gently places his hand over your arm that is on the armrest. Jesus is safe to be with. Can you allow yourself to feel his caring in the warmth of his touch? He now tells you that he is going to ask you something that is hard. . . . He asks you to share with him the deci-sions that you have made that you are not proud of. . . . Take this time to get everything off of your chest that weighs you down. [Pause.]

Listen as Jesus compassionately responds to what you have told him. [Pause.]

Jesus now invites you to share with him the decisions that you have not yet made—the ones that you are thinking about and may be confused about—so that he can help you. . . . Take this time to talk with Jesus some more and let him help you. [Pause.]

It is time for Jesus to leave you. He stands to go, but before he does, he places both of his hands in blessing upon your head. . . . Allow yourself to feel the warmth, encouragement, and love that he offers you. . . . Hear him say your name and that he loves you. . . . Listen as he says something important to you. Hear Jesus remind you to think before you act and then to choose wisely in all things, like Solomon. . . . What response do you give to Jesus? [Pause.]

Jesus warmly touches your shoulder as he moves into the aisle. . . . You see that he is smiling at you again. . . . You smile back. . . . You watch as he walks up the aisle and through the doors. . . . You sit back into your seat and remember this time you have just spent with Jesus. . . . You promise yourself that you will make good decisions that will keep you close to him. [Pause.]

Breathe in deeply . . . hold it . . . breathe out slowly and completely. Breathe in deeply . . . hold it . . . breathe out slowly and completely. Once more, breathe in deeply . . . hold it . . . breathe out slowly and completely. And when you are ready, you may open your eyes.

REFLECTION   Continue to play instrumental music. Ask the participants to reflect on the experience that they have just gone through.

Allow time for them to write their reflections on the following questions or questions similar to these:

- How did I feel to be in the empty movie theater and have Jesus sit beside me?
- What was my reaction to the woman who was willing to have the baby cut in half?
- What was my reaction to the real mother's choice to give up her baby?
- What did I think about Solomon's decision?
- What good decisions have I made? Did Jesus comment on them? If so, what did he say?
- How did I feel to name the decisions that I have made that I am not proud of? What was Jesus' response to them?
- When I discussed with Jesus the decisions that I am wrestling with, how did I feel? Do I have a better sense of what I should do? If so, what is it?
- Could I feel Jesus' hands on my head in blessing? What emotions did I feel at the time?
- Jesus tells me something before he leaves. What is it? What do I say back to him?
- What is the most important message or image that I am taking away with me from this prayer experience?

Invite and encourage the participants to share their reflections but do this without pressuring them to open up. Affirm their sharing.

ART EXPRESSION (OPTIONAL)

The art expression is an optional activity. It can be used in place of the reflection questions. If you decide to use one of these activities, prepare the art area before the group gathers.

Have ready at each place two small popcorn bags or boxes, or two small brown lunch bags with the word *Popcorn* printed on them; slips of paper that can be crumpled to look like popcorn or paper that has been pre-cut to look like popcorn; and pens or pencils. Also have a few staplers readily available.

It is best to give the following instructions before moving to the art area so as not to disrupt the quiet. Then invite the group to move quietly to the art area. Tell them that this is still part of the prayer experience. Continue playing instrumental music, as it helps with reverencing the moment.

On slips of paper, the participants are to write the decisions that they shared with Jesus, or any other decisions that they have made, that they are not proud of. Ask them to crumple the slips of paper and put them in one of the pop-corn bags or boxes. Staple the bag or box shut. Tell them that the slips of paper are like a bad batch of popcorn or the kernels that didn't pop.

On additional slips of paper, the participants are to write the good decisions that they have already made that they shared with Jesus. They can include other decisions that perhaps they didn't have time to tell Jesus. Encourage them to express how they felt after having made their decisions. They are to use as many slips of paper as they need. Next, they can write down any decisions that they want to make that they may or may not have told Jesus. Tell them to in-clude their thoughts and any advice that Jesus may have giv-en to them on the slips of paper. Tell them to use as many slips of paper as they need. Have them crumple all their slips of paper to look like popcorn and put them inside their other popcorn bag or box. Leave this bag or box open so that they can return to it at any time and remind themselves of their power to choose wisely.

Invite the participants to share their feelings about the wise choices that they have already made and those they hope to make in relation to the ones in the bag that they are not proud of. Encourage them to forget those that they can-not change and to concentrate on those for which they can now make wise choices. Allow time for sharing and affirm-ing each participant.

Tell them they can put their bags or boxes in a safe or visible place in their room to remind themselves of their promise to think before they act and then to choose wisely in all things.

CLOSING   Remind the group that they can always return to and spend time with Jesus in their imagination whenever they need to do so. Then, pray the following litany:

> *Litany Response*
> Help us to make wise decisions, Lord.
>
> In our families with our parents, adoptive parents, step-
>   parents, foster parents, grandparents, aunts,
>   uncles, and brothers and sisters of any kind . . .
> In our relationships with our friends . . .
> In the temptation to experiment with drugs, alcohol,
>   sex, or anything else that may be harmful to us . . .
> In our treatment of those we don't like or find different
>   from us . . .
> In our daily struggle to pray and do good acts . . .
>
> Together, in a sign of solidarity to offer support for one
> another's intentions and especially the decisions we
> have yet to make, let us pray the prayer Jesus taught us:
> "Our Father . . ."

Gifts ≈≈≈≈≈≈≈≈≈≈≈≈≈
Don't Bury Them

This challenging prayer experience, "Don't Bury Them," is based on the parable that Jesus told about the three servants who were entrusted with the responsibility of their master's wealth. It reminds us that we must develop our talents and make our efforts pleasing to the Master. After all, it is God who endows us with many riches.

THEME After you have given directions to the participants and set the tone for meditation, introduce the theme by saying something like the following:

> If we are to know the great gifts that God has entrusted to us individually, then we must spend time in a quiet place apart. We need to be still and listen to God's voice within us so that we might learn more deeply our own strengths and talents. Just as the two servants faithfully

and successfully invested their master's money, we, too, must faithfully and successfully develop our gifts. We cannot be like the third servant. We must remind ourselves, "Don't Bury Them!" We will grow more comfortable with ourselves and our talents if we willingly enter the hush of our quiet place.

OPENING Read aloud this opening prayer:

Creator God, help us to quiet down and enter this way of praying so that we can meet you in our imagination. Give us the openness to hear who we are and what talents and blessings are ours in our body, mind, spirit, and heart because of your great love for us. Grant us the courage to accept our gifts, and to develop and use them for the good of our own growth and that of others, and in so doing bring praise and glory to your holy name. Amen.

SCRIPTURE Read aloud Matthew 25:14–30, using a Bible.

SCRIPT Play the "Don't Bury Them" meditation on the accompanying recording or slowly and reverently read aloud the following script for the guided meditation. Play soft, instrumental background music.

Today you will enter the hush of your quiet place and meet Jesus in your imagination. First, you will begin by doing some deep-breathing exercises. When I say to, if you can, breathe in and out through your nose quietly during these exercises. Close your eyes and get comfortable. You will be relaxing your entire body.

Breathe in deeply . . . hold it . . . breathe out slowly and completely. Breathe in deeply . . . hold it . . . breathe out slowly and completely. Again, breathe in deeply . . . hold it . . . breathe out slowly and completely.

Allow your feet and ankles to relax. . . . Relax your legs . . . and your hips. . . . Remember to keep breathing in deeply and out slowly. Relax your stomach muscles . . . and now your chest. . . . Just relax. . . . Let your arms grow limp. . . . Relax your wrists, . . . your hands, . . . and your fingers. . . . Stay mindful of your breathing.

Allow your shoulders to become heavy. . . . Let all the tension drain from your shoulders. . . . Relax your neck, . . . your facial muscles, . . . and even your eyelids. . . . Just relax. . . . Breathe in deeply . . . hold it . . . breathe out slowly and completely. [Pause.]

It is a beautiful afternoon. The sun is shining, and it is warm, but not too warm. You are watching Jesus leave the steps of the Temple, and all of his Apostles are gathered around him. . . . You see Jesus stop in the middle of them. . . . It looks as if he has more to say to them. You watch as Jesus looks around and sees other people who are interested in hearing him. . . . Jesus waves his arms to bring others in closer to hear what he has to say. . . . Jesus looks over to where you are standing and he invites you to come in closer, too. . . . He is smiling at you as he does this. . . .

Hear Jesus say that he has a story to tell. . . . The crowd quiets down as they wait for him to speak. . . . You listen closely to Jesus. You know he is a good storyteller.

"Once there was a master who was going on a long journey. . . . He called three of his servants and gave them each a sizable amount of money according to the ability each had to be entrusted with it. . . ." Jesus looks around at all the people before he continues: "When he returned, the first and second servants had doubled the amount given them. . . . The master was well-pleased and gave them greater amounts of responsibilities. . . . The master told them to come and share in his joy. . . ." You watch as Jesus' face breaks into a huge grin as he says this.

But then you notice how serious he gets as he begins to finish the story. You suspect that he wants to say something very important through this parable. You listen even more intently.

"The third servant approached the master and reported that he was so afraid to lose the money that he buried it. . . . The master was angry and very disappointed in him. . . . He called him lazy and wicked because he had not even tried to invest his money. He was told to leave and could not share in his master's joy. . . ."

Jesus stops talking and looks around at the faces in the crowd. . . . You can tell people are thinking about the story Jesus told. You are thinking about it, too. But perhaps you are not sure what it means for you. All of a sudden, Jesus walks through the crowd toward you. . . . He is smiling again. Hear him say your name and "Come with me. Let us go for a walk together. . . ." Notice what you are feeling to have Jesus invite you to walk with him.

Listen as Jesus tells you that it is not really money that God, your heavenly Master, wants from you, but rather the gift of you growing into you! . . . Hear Jesus tell you that you are very special and like no one else. . . . Jesus also tells you that even though you possess a lot of different gifts in your body, mind, and spirit . . . the ones that come from your heart are most important—gifts like kindness, loyalty, thoughtfulness, and respect. . . . Listen as he shares with you the talents and blessings that have been given to you. . . . Some of them you know . . . but perhaps there are others that Jesus makes you aware of . . . especially the ones in your heart. Listen carefully. [Pause.]

He tells you that he hopes you will develop and use them to make you fully you and to give God greater glory. . . . Jesus tells you with such warmth and sincerity that you have been created with purpose. . . . His eyes hold such belief in you as he says: "And to fulfill that purpose, be faithful to the talents that have been given to you. . . . Don't bury them! . . . Then you will be invited to share in the Master's joy! . . ." You think for a moment about what Jesus is saying to you. [Pause.]

As you continue walking safely with Jesus, he places an arm about your shoulders. Hear him ask you to name those things in your life that you think keep you from being you—that stop you from developing or using your talents. . . . Jesus assures you that he is here to understand you. . . . He invites you to tell him everything. . . . You know you can feel safe with Jesus and trust him.

Take this time to share with Jesus all that is in your heart about how you feel about yourself and about other things happening in your life. [Pause.]

Jesus turns to face you now. . . . He looks deeply into your eyes. His voice is gentle but urgent. Listen as he promises you that he will be here with you . . . now and always . . . and that his belief in you will never die even if other people lose faith in you, or even if you lose faith in yourself.

. . . In return, promise Jesus that you will not bury the gifts of body, mind, heart, and spirit that you have been given. [Pause.]

Feel his excitement at your promise and if you can, receive the hug that he has for you. . . . Hear him whisper again: "Remember I am with you always and I believe in you. . . . You will share in the Master's joy!" [Pause.]

Thank Jesus for this time together. . . . Say your good-byes. . . . Watch Jesus return to the crowd . . . perhaps toward someone else who needs to be told—like you did—to use and celebrate what the Master has given as a gift.

Breath in deeply . . . hold it . . . breathe out slowly and completely. Breathe in deeply . . . hold it . . . breathe out slowly and completely. Once more, breathe in deeply . . . hold it . . . breathe out slowly and completely. And when you are ready, you may open your eyes.

REFLECTION   Continue to play instrumental music. Ask the participants to reflect on the experience that they have just gone through. Allow time for them to write their reflections on the following questions or questions similar to these:

• How did it feel to be part of the crowd listening to Jesus tell his story?

• What was my reaction on being invited to take a walk with Jesus?

• Can I name what I was feeling when Jesus started to tell me my gifts and talents?

• What did Jesus name as being gifts especially from my heart? Could I agree with him?

• What things did I share with Jesus that I think keep me from being me?

• Could I feel Jesus' hands on mine and his confidence in me?

• How does it make me feel to know that I will be invited to share in the Master's joy if I share my talents and gifts?

- Could I trust what Jesus was saying—that he'd always be there for me even when others let me down? that he'd be there even when I let myself down?
- What is the most special message or image that I will remember from this prayer experience?

Invite and encourage the participants to share their reflections but do not pressure them to open up. Affirm their sharing.

ART EXPRESSION (OPTIONAL)

The art expression is an optional activity. It can be used in place of the reflection questions. If you decide to use one of these activities, prepare the art area before the group gathers.

After the guided meditation, continue playing quiet music and ask the participants to move quietly to the art area. Remind them that this is still part of the prayer experience. Continue playing instrumental music, as it helps with reverencing the moment.

Art Expression 1

Set a place for each participant with a box of any size, small pieces of paper, pencils or pens, crayons or colored markers, colored ribbon, and scissors.

Instruct the participants to write their talents and gifts on the small pieces of paper and to place them inside the box. Using colors that express some of the talents or gifts that they talked about with Jesus, ask them to decorate the outside of the box with the crayons or markers. They can use symbols or words if need be; or, they can simply let the colors "do all the talking." Their name or nickname can also be drawn on the box for it contains much of who they are. They can also use colors, symbols, or words to describe their time with Jesus. Lastly, they are to use the ribbon to tie a big bow onto their "gift" box.

Art Expression 2

Set each place with one 11" x 17" sheet of art paper, rulers, colored crayons or markers, colored ribbon, and glue.

Instruct the participants to draw a large "gift" box on their art paper in any shape they want. Using colors to express how they feel about the gifts they have and the time spent with Jesus, they are to decorate their "gift" box with designs, symbols, or words that best describe what they are taking away with them from this prayer experience. Lastly, they are to fashion a bow out of ribbon to glue on their "gift" box.

After either art project, allow time for the sharing and affirming of each participant. Suggest that they put their "gift" box in a visible place in their room to remind them of Jesus' belief in them and of the belief they must have in themselves even when others lose faith in them. The "gift" box should remind them of their gifts and of the message "Don't Bury Them."

CLOSING Remind the participants that at any time they can return to their walk and visit with Jesus in their imagination. Then read aloud the following prayer:

> Creator God, thank you for making each one of us unique in body, mind, spirit, and heart. Help us to be true to the blessings of our gifts and talents by developing them fully. Guide us into using them for the good of ourselves and of others and especially to be pleasing to you. Make us aware of and appreciate the gifts and talents of others so that we may never put anyone else down. Help us to recall our gifts and talents during the times that we lose faith in ourselves and to remember the message "Don't Bury Them." As your children we lift this prayer up to you with confidence. Amen.

Obedience ≈ ≈ ≈ ≈ ≈ ≈ ≈ ≈ ≈ ≈ ≈
Do It Willingly

This encouraging prayer experience, "Do It Willingly," is based on the parable that Jesus told about the two sons who were asked by their father to go into the vineyards to help, and it is also rooted in Jesus' own experience of being called away from the Temple by his parents. It reminds us that we must be respectful and helpful to those with whom we live, whether we sometimes want to or not.

THEME   After you have given directions to the participants and set the tone for meditation, introduce the theme by saying something like the following:

> Sometimes it is important that we quiet ourselves in order to hear the Lord speak to us, especially about family life. We must reflect on our attitudes and actions

and on how these affect the people with whom we live. If we can be open and trusting to meet Jesus in the hush of our quiet place apart, then we will be ready to risk growing more mature in our relationships and actions at home.

OPENING Read aloud this opening prayer:

Lord, give us the gift of quiet so that we might settle ourselves down and block out any distractions in order to meet you in our imagination. Help us to face openly the attitudes and actions that we display in our family. Change our unwilling heart into an obedient heart that will help us "Do It Willingly" so that we may grow more mature in our love of you, of ourselves, and of one another. This is our prayer, which we ask you to hear and answer. Amen.

SCRIPTURE Read aloud Matthew 21:28–32 and Luke 2:41–52, using a Bible.

SCRIPT Play the "Do It Willingly" meditation on the accompanying recording or slowly and reverently read aloud the following script for the guided meditation. Play soft, instrumental background music.

Today you will enter the hush of your quiet place and meet Jesus in your imagination. First, you will begin by doing some deep-breathing exercises. When I say to, if you can, breathe in and out through your nose very quietly during these exercises. Close your eyes and get comfortable. You will be relaxing your entire body.

Breathe in deeply . . . hold it . . . breathe out slowly and completely. Breathe in deeply . . . hold it . . . breathe out slowly and completely.

Again, breathe in deeply . . . hold it . . . breathe out slowly and completely.

Allow your feet and ankles to relax. . . . Relax your legs . . . and your hips. . . . Remember to keep breathing in deeply and out slowly. Relax your stomach muscles . . . and now your chest. . . . Just relax. . . . Let your arms grow limp. . . . Relax your wrists, . . . your hands, . . . and your fingers. . . . Stay mindful of your breathing. . . .

Allow your shoulders to become heavy. . . . Let all the tension drain from your shoulders. . . . Relax your neck, . . . your facial muscles, . . . and even your eyelids. . . . Just relax. . . . Breathe in deeply . . . hold it . . . breathe out slowly and completely. [Pause.]

You are alone in a place that you like very much. It can be inside or outside. It can be in your room or den, at a friend's house, the football stadium, or a shopping mall; it can be in your favorite spot in nature—in a field, woods, mountains, or at the seashore. Wherever you want to be is fine, but know you are there safely alone. Just sit quietly and think about what makes this place important to you. . . . Now think about the people you live with. . . . How do you feel about them? . . . What have you done or not done for them lately? . . . What have they done or not done for you lately?

Someone is approaching your private place. . . . Don't be afraid, upset, or angry at being interrupted. It is Jesus. He wants to spend this time with you. Hear him say your name and tell you that he has looked forward to meeting you here by yourself. . . . Say hello to Jesus and invite him to sit down. . . . Hear Jesus say thank you. . . . When he is settled, Jesus turns to you and warmly asks you to tell him why this space is so special to you. . . . Tell Jesus. [Pause.]

Jesus now asks you to tell him about the people you live with and how you feel about them. . . . Don't worry about what you say to Jesus, . . . it is important to tell him everything. . . . Take this time to share with Jesus what your family life is like. Especially tell Jesus what your attitude and actions have been lately at home. . . . [Pause.] Listen as Jesus gently comments on what you have shared. . . . Hear the forgiveness and understanding in his voice. [Pause.]

Hear Jesus ask you to name something that you wanted done for you by a family member which wasn't, or which wasn't done as soon as you wanted it to be. Tell Jesus what it was, who let you down, and how you felt about it. . . . [Pause.]

Listen as Jesus tells you that he was let down, too. . . . [Pause.] What does he tell you? [Pause.]

Hear him tell you that it did not keep him from being faithful to the call God had for him. . . . Hear him tell you that he also wants you to be faithful to the call God has for you. . . . For himself, Jesus tells you that it started with being obedient when he was younger . . . and that it was hard to do but he did it.

Hear Jesus now ask you to describe a time when you were asked to do something and didn't or didn't do it right away. . . . Tell Jesus what that time was, who you let down, and how you felt about yourself. . . . Jesus lovingly forgives you for that time. . . . [Pause.]

Jesus reminds you of the two sons who were asked by their father to go into the vineyard to help. . . . One son said "no," but thought about it and went anyway; the other son said, "yes" but never went. . . . Jesus asks you which of the two sons did the will of their father. . . . Hear yourself answer Jesus. . . . Jesus tells you that you have to treat others the way you want to be treated. . . . Hear Jesus ask you if you can work on saying "yes" right away to those in your family who ask you to do something and if you can just "Do It Willingly" even when you don't want to? . . . Hear yourself respond to Jesus. . . . [Pause.]

Jesus moves so that he can stand and place both of his hands upon your head in blessing. . . . Jesus wants to give you strength and courage to live through the difficult times. He reminds you to bring both the good and bad of your life to prayer so that he can help you with everything. . . . You think about your family life and whom you need to react to better and love more. . . . You promise Jesus that you will make your life more obedient to God's plan by being more respectful and helpful to those at home. Jesus gives you a big grin and perhaps he even lovingly squeezes your shoulder. . . . It is clear that he is very proud of you.

Say your good-byes in whatever way is comfortable for you. . . . Watch as Jesus leaves your special place. Notice what you are feeling to have had Jesus join you . . . to have had Jesus all to yourself during this time. . . . Remember what you have promised.

Breathe in deeply . . . hold it . . . breathe out slowly and completely. Breathe in deeply . . . hold it . . . breathe out slowly and completely.

Once more, breathe in deeply . . . hold it . . . breathe out slowly and completely. And when you are ready, you may open your eyes.

REFLECTION

Continue to play instrumental music. Ask the participants to reflect on the experience that they have just gone through. Allow time for them to write their reflections on the following questions or questions similar to these:

- What place did I choose to be in? Why?
- How did I feel to have Jesus one-on-one with me?
- What did I tell Jesus about my family life?
- Could I honestly share with Jesus what my attitudes and actions have been lately? If so, what have they been?
- Who let me down? What was it about? How did I feel?
- How was Jesus let down? How did my knowing this make me feel?
- Have I let anyone down? What did I do or fail to do? How did I feel about myself afterward? Does it help to know that Jesus forgives me?
- Which of the two sons in the parable do I want to be like?
- In what ways can I be more aware of times when I can say "yes" and "do it willingly" to help others around me rather than be concerned only with doing my own thing?
- Could I feel Jesus' hands in blessing upon my head? Did that give me strength and courage for my life at home?
- To whom in my family will I react better? show more love?
- What is my promise to Jesus? Will this make my life more obedient to God's plan for me?
- What is the most special message or image that I am taking with me from this prayer experience?

Invite and encourage the participants to share their reflections but do not pressure them to open up. Affirm their sharing.

ART EXPRESSION
(OPTIONAL)

The art expression is an optional activity. It can be used in place of the reflection questions. If you decide to use one of these activities, prepare the art area before the group gathers.

After the guided meditation, invite the group to move quietly to the art area. Continue playing instrumental music, as it helps with reverencing the moment.

Art Expression 1

Set each place with pencils, black pens or fine-point black markers, a sheet of art paper, and a ruler.

Instruct the group to draw two comic strips with stick people characters (unless there are budding artists among them). The first comic strip is to depict the scene shared with Jesus in which their action or response disappointed a family member. The second comic strip is to depict a scene in which their attitude or action was positive and helpful to a family member or their home life.

Art Expression 2

Set each place with a sheet of art paper and crayons, colored markers, or watercolor or tempera paints. If paints are to be used, paintbrushes, paper toweling, newspaper, and cups of water will also be necessary.

Instruct the group to use colors to express their special place in which Jesus came to visit or they can draw the scene itself. Tell them to make sure that the colors they choose to use also express their feelings during their visit and or a particular message that they received during their time with Jesus.

After the art project, allow time for the sharing and affirming of each participant. Affirming can take several forms: nodding, inviting the participant to show his or her project so that everyone can see it, or saying such expressions as, "Thank you," "It took a lot of courage to share that," "How beautiful," "Good job," or "That seems to be something special you can remember."

Encourage the young people to put their art project in a visible place in their room to remind them of their time with Jesus and their promise to "Do It Willingly" when asked for help by a family member. Tell the participants that their art project should also be a reminder that Jesus is there for them and that all they have to do is reach out in prayer and talk to him.

CLOSING Remind the young people that they can return to their special place at any time and meet Jesus in their imagination. Suggest that perhaps they will need to do this to become more faithful in their "Do It Willingly" attitude, especially when home life is difficult. Then lead the following petitions:

Petition Response
Lord, help us to become more obedient and say "yes."

When a member of our family needs us to do something . . .
When our attitudes are not what you would want from us . . .
When our actions could be more helpful to home life . . .
When we should not do something that causes a problem in our family . . .
When we could be more like the first son in the parable . . .
When we let others down because it would be inconvenient for us to do what they need . . .
When we are thinking about whether or not to "Do It Willingly" . . .
When our heart could be more like yours, Jesus . . .

~~~~~~

Inner Blindness ~~~~~~~~~~~~~~~
I Want to See

This healing prayer experience, "I Want to See," is based on Jesus' cure of Blind Bartimaeus. It reminds us that we are lovable and forgivable no matter what our sins, what we hide, or what we are blind to.

THEME   After you have given directions to the participants and set the tone for meditation, introduce the theme by saying something like the following:

> There is a need to be in our quiet place apart so that we can focus on the areas of our life that need healing. Like Bartimaeus, we must reach out to the Lord of Light to cure the places in our life in which we have acted blindly or in which we have willingly hidden things that we are not proud of. If we can call out to the Lord as strongly as Bartimaeus did, then we shall receive the healing we need in the hush of our quiet place.

OPENING   Read aloud this opening prayer:

> Lord of Light, there are so many places in our life that we allow to remain in darkness due to selfishness and other sins that we desperately need you to bring us out of and into the light. Please be with us in a very real way as we enter this prayer time with you. Help us to look at the shabbiness of our attitudes and actions and choose to change them as did your new disciple, Bartimaeus. We lift this prayer up to you, our Lord of Light. Amen.

SCRIPTURE   Read aloud Mark 10:46–52, using a Bible.

SCRIPT   Play the "I Want to See" meditation on the accompanying recording, or slowly and reverently read aloud the following script for the guided meditation. Play soft, instrumental background music.

> Today you will enter the hush of your quiet place and meet Jesus in your imagination. First, you will begin by doing some deep-breathing exercises. When I say to, if you can, breathe in and out through your nose very quietly during these exercises. Close your eyes and get comfortable. You will be relaxing your entire body.
>
> Breathe in deeply . . . hold it . . . breathe out slowly and completely. Breathe in deeply . . . hold it . . . breathe out slowly and completely. Breathe in deeply . . . hold it . . . breathe out slowly and completely.
>
> Allow your feet and ankles to relax. . . . Relax your legs . . . and your hips. . . . Remember to keep breathing in deeply and out slowly. Relax your stomach muscles . . . and now your chest. . . . Just relax. . . . Let your arms grow limp. . . . Relax your wrists, . . . your hands,

. . . and your fingers. . . . Stay mindful of your breathing. . . .

Allow your shoulders to become heavy. . . . Let all the tension drain from your shoulders. . . . Relax your neck, . . . your facial muscles, . . . and even your eyelids. . . . Just relax. . . . Breathe in deeply . . . hold it . . . breathe out slowly and completely. [Pause.]

You are on a long, dusty, and winding road with Jesus, his Apostles, and a crowd of men, women, and children. . . . You are all leaving Jericho where Jesus has recently performed some miracles and done some preaching. The crowd is noisy and happy. . . . You can see Jesus up ahead of you, laughing and leaning in toward some of the younger people who are walking next to him. . . .

Suddenly you hear a man's voice crying out, "Jesus, Son of David, have pity. . . ." You hear it again. "Jesus, Son of David, have pity on me. . . ." It is so loud and insistent that the crowd begins to quiet so that they can hear and see what is going on. . . .

You, yourself, walk to the outside edge of the crowd so that you can find a way up front. . . . You stop when you see a beggar, dirty from the street dust, sitting in the ditch still calling out, "Son of David, have pity. . . ." You learn that people call him Blind Bartimaeus. . . . You can't help but stare at the way he looks with his eyes unseeing, his beard all straggly, and his old cloak tattered, worn in spots and with patches all over it. . . . His pockets are bulging. You wonder what he has hidden in those pockets and if he lives out of those pockets.

You see Jesus hold up one hand, directing the crowd to stop. You hear Jesus' voice say to two of his

Apostles near him, "Call him. Tell him to come. . . ." The Apostles James and John go to him. You hear John say encouragingly, "Get up, he is calling you. . . ."

You see Bartimaeus throw aside his cloak, jump up, and go over to Jesus with John guiding him through the crowd. . . . When he reaches Jesus, Bartimaeus half-kneels and then half-holds on to the clothes of Jesus that he doesn't see, but that he feels, rolling the material between two of his fingers. This doesn't seem to bother Jesus. Instead, Jesus places one of his own hands over the frail hand that clings to his garment. . . . You watch as Jesus tenderly looks at him. . . . Warmly, you hear his voice as he asks Bartimaeus, "What do you want me to do for you? . . ."

Stretching his face towards Jesus' voice, Bartimaeus replies hopefully, "Master, I want to see. . . ."

Jesus grips the hand that is holding onto his clothes and begins to pull Bartimaeus upright. . . . Powerfully, yet softly, you hear Jesus say to the beggar, "Go on your way; your faith has saved you. . . ." Blind Bartimaeus looks stunned. With his hands he shades his eyes from the bright daylight, you can see that his hands are shaking and tears are beginning to make streaks down his dirty face. For a moment, it looks as though he's memorizing the face of the one who has healed him. . . . Then, rubbing his eyes, he starts shouting: "I can see! I can see!" He straightens up and it appears that a great burden has been lifted from his shoulders. You sense that it is due to more than just the return of his eyesight. Then the overwhelming joy that he feels makes him jump into a Jewish dance and people are clapping and shouting with him. . . . Even Jesus joins in!

There's a moment when Bartimaeus quiets and turns his head, straining to look at Jesus and get close to him. . . . But his complete joy at being cured has excited the entire crowd so much that he can't get anywhere near him. . . . You keep your eyes on Bartimaeus and again he struggles to reach Jesus, who has begun to be swallowed up by the crowd. Over the heads of everyone, you notice their eyes meet and a look of great love and gratitude pass between them. . . . It is a look that, perhaps, you wish you shared with Jesus.

The crowd in its excitement begins to push and shove. . . . Bartimaeus is now lost to you. But suddenly, Jesus is next to you. . . . His head is leaning in close to yours. You hear his voice lovingly say your name. He looks gently into your eyes and says: "It is time to talk about the moments you have been blind. . . . It is time to talk about the things that you hide that weigh you down. . . ."

You think for a while, as you continue walking, about all of the ways you have acted blindly—the ways you have sinned and been in a darkness that made you feel lost and sitting in a ditch like Bartimaeus. . . . You think about your actions and attitudes in your relationships with your family members, . . . your teachers, . . . your friends, . . . and all the kids you don't treat as friends. . . . You think about your prayer life and how your relationship is doing with God. . . . You think about things that you did not do but should have . . . and the things that you did do but shouldn't have. [Pause.]

You start to tell Jesus about the stuff that has happened that makes your life sometimes look and feel like Bartimaeus' cloak—all torn up in places, with patched areas and with pockets in which are hidden shame or fears or sorrows. . . . What is it that you need to get rid of in order to throw aside your cloak, jump up, be healed, and see with new eyes? You tell Jesus everything. [Pause.]

Listen carefully as Jesus gently responds to you and all that you have shared. [Pause.]

Hear Jesus tell you that you are loved, . . . that you are forgiven for all that has been that you are not proud of. . . . See Jesus give you the same special look that he gave Bartimaeus. Notice what you are feeling in this moment. Hear Jesus tell you that as long as you remain close to him as your Light, you will not be blind. . . . You will not have heavy things that weigh you down. . . . You will not have things you feel you have to hide. . . . Jesus places a hand upon your cheek and once again, looks into your eyes. Hear Jesus tell you something that is just for you. What does he say? You want to remember this forever. [Pause.]

It is time for Jesus to walk among others in the crowd now. Say whatever you need to to Jesus and share any affection that is comfortable for you. Know that you shall never forget the warmth you feel for having been with Jesus. Allow him now to disappear into the crowd. . . . Continue to walk quietly as you remember this time that you have spent with Jesus.

Breath in deeply . . . hold it . . . breathe out slowly and completely. Breathe in deeply . . . hold it . . . breathe out slowly and completely. Once more, breathe in deeply . . . hold it . . .

breathe out slowly and completely. And when you are ready, you may open your eyes.

REFLECTION Continue to play instrumental music. Ask the participants to reflect on the experience that they have just gone through. Allow time for them to write their reflections on the following questions or questions similar to these:

- What was it like for me to be part of the crowd walking with Jesus?
- What was my first reaction to hearing and seeing Blind Bartimaeus?
- What did I think about Jesus asking James and John to bring Bartimaeus over?
- Describe what I felt when I saw Jesus treat Bartimaeus so tenderly and cure him. Could I have treated a beggar tenderly?
- Could I feel myself get caught up in the excitement of the crowd?
- How did I feel when I noticed the special look pass between Jesus and Bartimaeus?
- Was I glad to have my own personal time with Jesus? Why or why not?
- What did I name for Jesus that are areas of inner blindness or darkness caused by sin? What are some of the things that I keep hidden due to fear, shame, or sorrow? What things have made me feel like I've been in a ditch like Bartimaeus?
- How did I feel to have Jesus' understanding and forgiveness? Did I feel that I could throw aside my cloak of burdens, jump up, and be healed? Can I see with new eyes? Explain.
- What does Jesus tell me that is just for me? How does it make me feel?
- Do I think I can remember the warmth of Jesus' hug?
- Did I need to say something to Jesus before he left? If so, what?
- What is the most special message or image that I am taking with me from this prayer experience?

ART EXPRESSION
(OPTIONAL)

The art expression is an optional activity. It can be used in place of the reflection questions. If you decide to use one of these activities, prepare the art area before the group gathers.

After the guided meditation, invite the group to move quietly to the art area. Continue playing instrumental music, as it helps with reverencing the moment.

Art Expression 1

At each place, have two sheets of 9" x 12" art paper, a pencil, crayons or colored markers, scissors, and glue.

Instruct the participants to draw and cut out their version of a cloak from the first sheet of art paper. Tell them to mark it, cut it, or patch it in ways and with colors that symbolize the shabby areas of their life that they shared with Jesus. Have them glue down only their cloak's shoulder area onto the other art paper. Tell them to lift up their cloak and write underneath it or in the "pockets" those shabby or sinful areas that are depicted by the markings on their cloak.

Then instruct the participants to use colors or symbols all around their cloak that express what feelings they experienced after witnessing the cure of Bartimaeus and spending this time with Jesus, how they felt to throw off their cloak, and how their life will change due to this prayer time.

Please note: This meditation has previously been used as an examination of conscience and this art expression has accompanied individuals during the Sacrament of Reconciliation for a real and valuable experience of "throwing off their shabby cloak and seeing with new eyes."

Art Expression 2

At each place, have a half-sheet of black construction paper and a full sheet of white art paper, a pencil, crayons or colored markers, scissors, and glue.

Instruct the participants to cut out the shape of an eye from the black construction paper and glue it onto one half of the white art paper. This is to symbolize a blind eye. Next they are to draw a seeing eye on the other half. Around the blind eye, they are to use colors, words, or symbols to express how they have sinned and been in darkness. Around the seeing eye, they are to express what or how this prayer experience has taught them to see with new eyes and how this will help them change their attitudes or actions.

After either art expression, allow the participants time for sharing. Accept and affirm all responses. Suggest that they put their art expression someplace safe in their room so that when they see it, it will remind them of this time they spent with Jesus and that they are lovable and forgivable despite their sins, their inner blindness, and what they have hidden or done in the past. Tell them it should recall the expression, "I Want to See."

CLOSING   Remind the young people that at any time they can go for a walk with Jesus in their imagination and seek healing and help. Then lead the following thanksgiving litany:

> *Litany Response*
> Lord of Light, we thank you for taking away the darkness.
>
> For the times you have given us your love and forgiveness . . .
> During moments that you have helped us to see more clearly how we should act with our friends . . .
> To know what to do when we want to do what we shouldn't . . .
> To know that we can follow through when we should do something that we don't want to do . . .
> When we change our attitude within our family . . .
> In giving us the example of the beggar, Blind Bartimaeus . . .
> For the warmth we received from your tenderness and hug . . .
> To help us give over fears and shame and develop our prayer life with you . . .
> For taking away our inner blindness . . .

ACKNOWLEDGMENTS
(continued)

To Aggie I express my loving appreciation for her active support and expressed belief in me and my work. Her endorsement has been invaluable and has spurred this fourth manuscript to joyful completion.

A heartfelt thank you to my editor, Fr. Robert Stamschror, whose kind ways and vested interest in me personally and professionally make working with him an absolute pleasure, and to his team, I express much appreciation for another "painless" publication well done . . . with special thanks to Karen J. Doyle, friend and illustrator, whose artwork depicts the warmth and realness of Jesus' presence in our life.

To my gifted musician, Barry Russo, whose instrumental pieces on the synthesizer are a poignant interpretation of, and addition to, the guided recordings, I am deeply grateful for his sharing of his inspired talent once again.

Recording with Anthony "Barrel" Marrapese of Reel to Real Recording Studio, Cranston, Rhode Island, is such an enjoyable experience that I can only express my gratitude to him and look forward to the next time work brings us together.

And to those other blessings in my life who nurture and sustain me: Isabel, Shirley, Eileen, Cheryl, Alycia and Pete, Jean, Sr. Mary George, Pauline, Fr. Jude, Aunt Mary, B. J. and Bob, Lisa, Sue, Jon, Kathy, Agnes L., Libby, Belle, the Doyles, Drea, Andre, Tom, Fred, Mercymount faculty and students, and those who have hired me for retreat work—you are treasured gifts. Thank you.

Other titles in the
A Quiet Place Apart Series
available from Saint Mary's Press

Each of the titles in this series has a leader's guide and recordings of the meditation scripts. The leader's guide contains directions for preparing the meditations, the meditation scripts, and suggestions for follow-up after the meditations. The audiocassette and the compact disc contain high-quality recordings of the meditation scripts against a background of original music.

Guided Meditations for Adults: Salvation, Joy, Faith, Healing

Jane E. Ayer

These guided meditations for adults are on the themes of salvation, joy, faith, and healing.

Leader's guide: 0-88489-393-6, 7½ x 9¼, 44 pages, stitched, $9.95
Audiocassette: 0-88489-394-4, 90 minutes, $8.95
Compact disc: 0-88489-424-X, 90 minutes, $14.95

Guided Meditations for Youth on Personal Themes

Jane E. Arsenault

These guided meditations are on the themes of new life, discipleship, self-esteem, and secrets.

Leader's guide: 0-88489-347-2, 7½ x 9¼, 46 pages, stitched, $8.95
Audiocassette: 0-88489-354-5, 90 minutes, $7.95

Guided Meditations for Youth on Sacramental Life

Jane E. Arsenault and Jean R. Cedor

These guided meditations are on the four sacraments of baptism, confirmation, the Eucharist, and reconciliation.

Leader's guide: 0-88489-308-1, 7½ x 9¼, 40 pages, stitched, $8.95
Audiocassette: 0-88489-309-X, 90 minutes, $7.95

"The guided meditation used at our eighth-grade retreat was superb. The students' reactions were highly positive. Some said that through this type of reflection they were able to be more in touch with their own feelings and their relationship to God." **Charles Moreira,** teacher, Saint Brendan School, Riverside, RI, and CRE, Saint Margaret's Parish, East Providence, RI

"'Let's meditate again' was the students' response the day following their first guided meditation experience during their retreat with Jane Ayer. These guided meditations are a wonderful opportunity for youth to experience prayer in a deep, personal way." **Miriam McBurnie,** RSM, School of Saint Leo the Great, Pawtucket, RI